paper
craft kit

Materials and Instructions for
Beautiful Handmade Paper Creations

BY Sidd Murray-Clark

CHRONICLE BOOKS
SAN FRANCISCO

ISBN 0-8118-4828-0

Design by Blake Kahan
Typeset in Farao, Filosofia, and Avenir

Manufactured in China

Chronicle Books endeavors to use
environmentally responsible paper
in its gift and stationery products.

Distributed in Canada by
Raincoast Books
9050 Shaughnessy Street
Vancouver, B.C. V6P 6E5

10 9 8 7 6 5 4 3 2 1

Chronicle Books LLC
85 Second Street
San Francisco, CA 94105
www.chroniclebooks.com

contents

paper tales & moving words

● ●

Picture the verdant banks of the ancient river Nile some 4,000 years ago,
where great swaths of papyrus beds flourished. It was here that the ancient
people of Egypt devised one of the first kinds of paper material. The word
paper comes from the Greek word for papyrus (*papyros*). The Greeks found that
the leaves of this reedy plant, when stripped into fine strands, could be woven
into mats. They then hammered the sheets flat, releasing the natural glue in
the leaves, and laid them out to dry in the sun. These woven "mats" were an
offshoot from other uses of woven leaves, like baskets and roofs for huts.

A few hundred years later, in another part of the world, the ancient
culture of the Mayans also developed a surface for their writing. Their raw
material came from the fig tree. They boiled pieces of its bark until it became
soft. Overlapping these pieces, they hammered them together in a single
mesh, which when dried became a kind of paper they called *amatyl*.

At the same time, in India and Southeast Asia, palm and birch trees were
being used for writing material. The broad palm leaves and skin-like birch bark
were sewn together with thin strips of leather to make some of the first books.

Early writing surfaces didn't just come from plant materials. Ever since
man first wrapped himself in the skins of animals, he has used this natural
resource of a strong and flexible material for myriad things—from housing to
boats to body armor—but also for a writing surface. Parchment, the first form
of animal-skin paper, was developed in ancient Persia by splitting sheepskins,
and smoothing the surface with a pumice stone.

MAKING OUR MARK

The search for materials on which to record our lives goes back to
prehistory. The history of communication is interwoven with the story of
making marks, hieroglyphs, pictograms, and words. Early man scratched,

drew, and daubed records and symbols of the hunt on ancient cave walls and carved images of his life on stone, calabash, and bone. Scholars agree that these early depictions of life, though awkward, may have held a more profound significance for our ancestors than as mere records of daily life. In reproducing these images, early peoples were seeking to endow themselves with greater powers in the struggle to survive and understand. And in years to come, these markings would evolve into a written language.

THE POWER OF THE WRITTEN WORD

As early man's lifestyle developed into settlements and eventually into civilizations, the writing down of sacred law or beliefs seems to have given most cultures a deeper worth. In addition, writing down such things allowed for more permanent records to be kept for future generations. Even now, in the modern world of telecommunication, we call for a written document to seal an agreement.

In early times these significant records, religious teachings, and documentations were inscribed into various hard surfaces for their safekeeping. Stone tablets may have been relatively permanent and stable but they were heavy, cumbersome, and difficult to transport. Lighter and more manageable surfaces on which to write were needed. The versions of paper mentioned earlier—parchment and tree leaves—were already a great advance from clay or wax tablets; however, it was the discovery of plant pulp that would irrevocably change the story of paper.

Around 250 B.C. a Chinese man by the name of Meng Tien invented a paintbrush made of camel's hair. At this time literacy was growing in China, and as a result more and more people were learning to write. The writing materials used at the time were silk, clay tablets, or linen and while these three were preferable to stone tablets, another more portable and versatile material was needed.

Some 350 years later, in 105 A.D., a Chinese eunuch and imperial court official named Tsar Lin invented a thin material made from macerated vegetable fibers. By settling this pulp on porous molds or trays, he created the first true paper, with a felt-like surface. In its early form the pulp was made from tree bark, hemp, rags, and even fishnets, but it would soon be refined and become the favored writing surface throughout China. The Chinese culture placed great value on literature, and the administration of its burgeoning bureaucracy created a great deal of paperwork, both prime uses for the new invention.

This breakthrough was followed a few hundred years later by the invention of solid ink, which was powdered charcoal in the form of cakes or sticks. These blocks could be dissolved in water to make liquid ink for writing. Before this development, ink had consisted of a mixture of soot and oil. The new ink was much smoother and more consistent and is still used today in calligraphy and brush painting. We have evidence of the first paper money from this time printed with this ink. It was called "spirit money" because it was placed with the dead for their journey to the other realm. The spirit money was later established as an actual currency around 660 A.D., during the Tang Dynasty under Emperor Kao Tsung.

PAPER TRAVELS

It took 500 years (until 605 A.D.) for the secrets of papermaking to travel east from China to Korea. Then, in 610 A.D. a Buddhist monk named Dokyo traveled from Korea and brought papermaking to Japan. At first, Japanese paper production was centered in the capital towns and was mainly created for government and temple use, but by the eleventh century A.D. it had begun to spread to the rural regions where abundant raw materials could be found. Local plants such as *kozo* added new strength to the fibers of the paper brought from Korea.

The Ino-Cho region of Japan is perhaps the most famous of the early paper-making regions in the country, due to several key innovations. Records say that originally papers from this area were used by the imperial court for religious purposes, and near the end of the sixteenth century color-dyed paper was produced here for the first time in Japan. In 1860 larger sheets of paper were produced in Ino-Cho, including a resinous type on which the ink of fountain pens did not smudge. From here the techniques were passed on to other areas, and each area's paper became distinct in some way; for example, in Iiyama the fibers used to make *Uchiyama* paper were bleached by laying them out in the snow. *Inshu* paper from Saji has a particularly fine quality, the result of adapting many techniques from other areas. The beautiful translucent papers for *shoji* and *fusuma* screens were developed in Saji, and this led to the creation of the famous artists' paper called *mitsumata*.

The primary religions of Japan, Shintoism and Buddhism, hold a deep reverence for life and nature, and the Japanese people have a deep respect for craft because it is a pure expression of this essential quality. Ordinary everyday objects become not only useful but also uplifting to the human spirit. It was in this culture that papermaking first emerged as a real art. In Shintoism, paper is still a symbol of purity, and folded paper is used for talismans and in prayers to mark a sacred spot. There is a temple today in Tokushima, in which the god of paper *Amenohiwashi no Mikoto* is enshrined.

WASHI

Washi, which literally means "paper" in Japanese, is a collective word for many different types of paper produced in diverse areas in Japan. Different districts developed their own paper using the abundant materials available locally. The baste fibers, or raw material, were taken mainly from mulberry bark and certain shrubs, though hemp, bamboo, and even rice straw were used.

Washi was used in many other applications besides as a surface for writing and painting. Paper became synonymous with such things as the fan, the lantern, and sliding door panels (known as *shoji*). Oiled paper was used for umbrellas and the sails of boats. When lacquered with the sap from a sumac tree, paper hardened and could be formed into bowls, ornaments, and even furniture. This lacquer craft became such a big export to Europe that it was to become known as *Japan-ware*. Many of the basic techniques of today's paper craft originate from this creative culture.

CHARTS WEST

Such a significant discovery as paper could not stay in Asia forever and, in 751 A.D., some Saracens uncovered the secret. These marauding Arabs had attacked the ancient Central Asian city of Samarkand, which had its own paper mill, and forced some captive Chinese soldiers to reveal the secret method of making paper. The Arab culture was a civilized one and they soon appreciated the far-reaching possibilities of this humble material. The influence of the Arab world extended far west across the whole Mediterranean basin, and so the spread of paper begin to move westward through the world of Islam. By the time it arrived in the Moorish courts of Spain in the mid 900s, it had taken the place of vellum and parchment as the preferred writing material.

From here the whole of Europe was soon to know about this simple but versatile material. Evidence shows that paper was first used in England around 1300 and the Fabriano mill was first in production some 50 years earlier in Italy. By 1400, parchment in Europe had also largely been replaced by paper.

THE MOVING WORD

Meanwhile, back in Asia, the Chinese had invented the first movable type. The scholar Wang Chieh apparently made the earliest known printed book, the *Diamond Sutra*, in 868. Playing cards were block printed as early as 969, and this basic technique of printing was to be adapted to movable type by the scholar Pi Sheng.

The Chinese and other Asian languages use pictograms rather than an alphabet. The pictograms (characters) are made up of parts called radicals, and the radicals can be arranged in a number of different ways to create different characters (words), making a nearly infinite number of combinations and resultant characters. So in its early form the method of movable type would prove far more useful to other languages with simpler alphabets (for example, in English there are only 26 different letters to be combined to make words). It was not until 1423 that this method arrived in Europe, and the first printing press with movable type was set up by Johann Gutenberg in Germany.

The book publishing that followed the invention of movable type not only required high-quality paper to match the importance of the books, but also an acceptance of the new printing methods of illustration such as etching, wood-cutting, and engraving. It is said that Rembrandt, the 17th century Dutch master, made some of his etching on a pure white paper that came from the Orient. It has now been analyzed as washi paper from Japan.

Until movable type was invented, paper had been used primarily for exclusive religious manuscripts. The printing press allowed the widespread dispersion of knowledge and learning. As books became more and more popular, the demand for paper grew. The raw materials for papermaking were cotton, linen rags, and even old sailcloth, but by the 18th century the supply of these fabrics could not meet the demand of papermaking. When William Rittenhouse and William Bradford arrived from Europe to Germantown, Pennsylvania, to start their papermaking mill, they found scant supply of these fabrics. It is reported that even Egyptian mummies were imported and their rags used for making paper. Every rag was conserved, and soldiers even tore up precious books to serve as wadding for their guns rather than use rags. Little did they know that the Mayans living further south had discovered wood pulp for papermaking over a thousand years earlier.

WATCHING WASPS

In 1719 a French apiarist named Rene-Antoine Ferchault de Reaumur was observing some wasps when he noticed that they collected wood chips to make their paper-like nests. This observation led, some 80 years later, to the invention of a crude machine to grind wood into fibers. In the following century the machine was refined, and other technical issues, such as the removal of resins, were resolved. With this ready and plentiful source of fiber, and a streamlined purifying process using sulfites, the raw material for paper took a huge leap.

The method of setting the plant pulp by hand in latticed trays made from fine strips of wood or from woven fabric had remained unchanged for almost a millennium. Even though machines would replace this age-old method, they often imitated the handmade process.

These changes led to a leap in production and a rapid exploration of the versatility of paper. Paper began to be laminated for various uses, and media developed for papier-mâché and Japan-ware. As manufacturing improved, paper was applied to a wide variety of utilitarian and creative possibilities. For example, modern technology has developed paper for automobile brakes, heat shields, and even to suppress radio interference in cell phones. It is now a $1 billion industry involving every kind of paper and its allied products.

SACRED PAPER

Though paper is ubiquitous in our world today, and we hardly think about it when we use it, it wasn't always this way. When paper was a rare and precious material, it was held in great respect, even taking on a religious significance. Costumes, adornments, and decorations were made from amatyl, a bark paper, and worn by the Mayan priests for their elaborate ceremonies and sacred dances. In China it was used in funerals, by shaping sacred symbols out of paper, which were then burned, and also in the home by pasting on the walls images of Taoist and Buddhist gods on paper, for protection.

And in some cultures today, paper is still used for symbolic purposes. Papier-mâché is used to make ceremonial masks in Tibet. In the Shinto tradition, as a symbol of purity, paper is folded in a special way and hung in trees at the shrine as an offering of prayer. In our own daily lives, words or art presented on a fine paper have a special and rarified quality, as if those precious origins have come full circle. Now an important document, a résumé, or certificate is often presented on premium paper to draw attention to its significance.

MANY PAPERS, MANY USES

The chronicle of paper is also the story of creative and unusual applications equal to the versatility of the material, and dates back to the simple use of leaves and foliage as container, shelter, or clothing. There is still evidence of this in many Asian countries that have remained connected to their environment and origin. Some examples are food served on banana leaves, baskets and hats woven into the most complex design, and whole styles of architecture developed using indigenous plants and trees.

Out of this relationship with his environment, humankind has created the world of craft and art, including the development of paper and paper-like materials. By sorting and blending natural materials, he developed more practical and controllable sheets to work with. In the various climate regions and continents, the environment and indigenous plant life influenced or determined the nature of these discoveries and the uses to which they were applied. Many great civilizations have developed along rivers. So too did paper, and the origins of papyrus and washi paper bear witness to this. For example, papyrus, in its abundance along the Nile, not only gave the Egyptians a building material for their boats and houses, and even a source of food from its roots, but also a form of paper for the civilizing world that was to last for almost 4,000 years.

In early times such stuff seemed magical or from another world, and these paper-like products often took on a religious significance worldwide. It is interesting to note that the paper with the most value nowadays is money, and we live in a consumer society where paper is a major disposable.

We find records from the ancient Mayan culture written in their accordion-like books, or *codex*, and see it in their sacred costumes and adornments such as paper crowns, flags, stoles, and banners. Even today some tribes still practice certain magic rituals in this elaborate sacred garb made from the same amatyl or bark paper. At the same time it was applied to a variety of utilitarian purposes.

Due to paper's organic nature, only some paper products from the past have survived, but what does endure tells a remarkable tale of human ingenuity. We know that paper has been used for the most delicate purposes, such as fans, and the most robust, such as a dome on a building. Its skin-like flexibility and strength has lent itself to boat building and to clothing, to umbrellas and to architectural beams. This plasticity can be treated in different ways stretching the possibilities even further. In Korea paper was treated with oil to make floor coverings and even raincoats!

Paper can also be made thin and translucent to transmit light. This quality is probably best known for its application in the shoji of Japan.

TODAY'S PAPER

Concerns and renewed awareness about ecology and our environment are leading us to take a fresh look at the old handmade methods of papermaking. At the same time this physical reconnection with the process and material is cultivating creativity and extending the role of paper in our lives in a renewed way.

Why is it that when we want to remember something or explain it, we often turn to paper to write on? It is almost as if paper has become part of our communication process. Some scientists believe we even think in words and pictures, which appear on the screen of our minds. These days, as computer screens often take the place of the physical display of our thoughts, ideas, and messages on paper, we can take another look at paper and appreciate it for what it is.

In a world of mass production, we easily take many products for granted. We can lose touch with the intrinsic qualities of everyday materials, which are often rich and inspiring by themselves. Artists are constantly concerned and involved with their materials, and challenge the medium they work in. By returning to the raw materials of papermaking, contemporary artists are discovering the tremendous versatility of this material.

At each step of the papermaking process, there are creative possibilities and alternatives in the type of raw material, which in turn determine its final effects. The action of overlaying, weaving, and blending different fibers is as old as papermaking. Paper pulp itself can be cast, molded like clay, sprayed, poured, spun and woven, sawed, carved, and embellished in many ways.

Paper is paradoxical in that it can be both delicate and strong. It can be made soft, translucent, sinewy, or rock hard. In this wide range of potential, artists and creators are exploring new horizons. Artists now accept paper as more than just a support for their creative expression. Paper can be the medium itself.

The Japanese architect Shigeru Ban has examined the extraordinary tensile applications of paper and is building whole structures from it.

Frank Gehry, the groundbreaking designer/architect, found a whole new application for that humble packing material called corrugated cardboard, and he has designed wonderful flowing shaped furniture out of this everyday item.

Paper as clothing has been around for millennia, and Issey Miyake, the Japanese fashion designer, is constantly redefining its use in his creations.

The sculptor Isamu Noguchi took *chochin*, the paper lanterns of fishermen in Japan, and expanded these humble lamps into luminous sculptures.

FOR PAPER'S SAKE

Some artists today have returned to the pure art of papermaking as their inspiration. Their art is born out of the integrity of the material itself. Instead of being simply a useful product, paper can be beautiful by itself. These artists are not limited to a paper mill or the repetitiveness of manufactured paper, but build unique objects from the actual pulp and fibers. Simple paper, in creative hands, can transform an ordinary object. Handmade papers, arranged aesthetically, can become an art piece to enhance the atmosphere of a room with its natural beauty.

Why do we wrap gifts in beautiful paper? We like to make something special to give to a friend or loved one. This takes us back to the beginnings of paper, when it was revered for its unique qualities and used for sacred and respectful occasions.

This humble material has a warm attractive character in its texture and form. A beautiful paper, like a rich and interesting fabric, invites us to touch and play with it. Its feel inspires us to work it with our hands and explore its qualities. Its nature evokes delight and the inspiration to create or enhance something with it. It has an inherent aesthetic quality, and sometimes just the presence of a handmade sheet of paper is enough to bring beauty to our lives.

We can explore this rediscovered appreciation of the simple and inherent quality of paper through many avenues. The history of paper is rich with examples from ancient artifacts, enduring folk craft, and modern innovations. You can find these treasures in books, on the Internet, and in craft stores and galleries. See the Resources list on page 63 for more information.

techniques
& materials

Paper as we generally know it has been around for more than 2,000 years. Throughout its evolution into the media we know today, the manipulation of paper into utilitarian and decorative forms was the origin of the modern-day art of paper craft. This kit is an opportunity to explore and create using this simple but versatile material.

Paper now comes in many varieties and qualities, from "run-of-the-mill" to handmade. It can be delicate, like the petal of a flower, or robust, even waterproof. It has been developed to suit many purposes, and also to delight and decorate our lives!

In this kit you will find a selection of papers and 10 projects to create, introducing you to the delightful world of paper craft. Each project is carefully described with a simple introduction and easy-to-follow instructions. You can create each project as a personalized gift, as artwork for your home, or simply as a jumping-off point to explore your own ingenuity in the world of paper craft.

As discussed below, the basic methods behind paper craft are cutting, bending, folding, and scoring, as well as paper decoration and assembly. You will get to use these methods in each of the projects in your kit.

TECHNIQUES
Paper Sculpting

A simple piece of paper comes alive when we apply craft techniques such as bending, folding, scoring, and cutting. These basic actions can be combined to create a wide range of exciting possibilities. By cutting, scoring, and bending paper, you can create interesting shapes and effects. The results can be beautiful in their own right, or they can be made to be representative of other images or ideas.

Many countries around the world have a tradition of paper folding, the most famous of which is the art of origami from Japan. The folded paper napkins we sometimes find at our table in a restaurant, or folded paper party hats at a child's birthday party, have their origins in origami. As an art it continues to evolve, and is practiced by great artists and even engineers, as they explore the turning of a flat surface into a three-dimensional form.

Paper sculpting was all the rage in eighteenth-century England, where artisans created an illusion of three dimensions by shaping paper and imposing various forms of relief. Paper folding was used as a teaching tool in nineteenth-century German kindergartens, and the Bauhaus later used it in their commercial design curriculum. Architects and designers have used cardboard in this way since the early twentieth century to make their models and maquettes. More recently, they have used paper to construct actual buildings, real furniture, and even handbags.

There are also many cultural traditions surrounding the technique of paper cutting that have developed into an art form. Examples of the intricacy and complexity of fine delicate patterns and perforations cut out of paper range from Javanese shadow puppets to Mexican wall hangings (*papel picado*) to Victorian portraiture.

Today, many household objects are based on paper folding and cutting, such as envelopes, paper bags, and even cartons. If you take an empty milk carton and carefully break the glued seams, it will open up into a flat piece of card. Through this example it is easy to see that this everyday container has its origin in the ancient tradition of origami.

Paper Decoration

A sheet of paper can become the basis for many decorative effects. The pliant and giving nature of its surface will respond to numerous media and methods. Pressing into the surface of paper in different ways produces varied and interesting results. By pressing a shape or design from the back of the paper, you are **EMBOSSING** your paper.

You can make marks on paper with objects too. If you apply paint to the surface of paper with a stamp or found object, this is called **STAMPING**. There are many ready-made stamps available, but you can also make your own from objects such as a potato or sponge. The type of paper, the nature of the stamp, and the quality of paint determine the final visual effect. Many printing methods such as block printing, etching, and gravure are based on this principle.

There are other ways to print on paper without using a stamp of any kind. To create a **MONOPRINT**, put your paint or ink on a hard surface and then press the paper down on the paint. The Japanese developed a kind of printing called *orizomegami*, in which paper is folded and then dye applied to its different parts. When the paper is opened, a beautiful random print emerges.

STENCILING allows you to repeat motifs and designs. A stencil is a thin sheet of stiff material, such as card or thin plastic, which you can cut shapes out of (though often stencils come precut). These shapes can be transferred onto another surface (such as the sheets of paper included in this kit) by placing your stencil on the paper or card and then drawing or painting inside these shapes. Once you have created a stencil (or procured a ready-made one), you can create many patterns and repeated effects.

PAINTING paper has long been a fascination of artists. In ancient China, for example, people painted and wrote with brush and ink. As a result, their paper needed to be somewhat absorbent. On the other hand, Europeans wrote with quill pens, so their paper needed to have a smoother and harder finish. With the advent of fine illustrative printing techniques in Europe in the sixteenth century, printmakers required more specialized types of paper.

Artists have always sought new surfaces on which to paint, challenging papermakers to find new possibilities. With so many types of paper now available, you can experiment in as many ways as you can imagine. For example, when you play with paint on paper, you may at first want to use a brush, but don't forget that flicking, splashing, rubbing, spilling, and dyeing also create fabulous effects!

Paper Treatment and Assembly

COLLAGE is a collective term that describes different ways to treat and assemble flat pieces of paper.

One such process, in which cut paper is affixed to some object, is called **DECOUPAGE**. This method started in the seventeeth century as a form of decorating furniture and other household items. Influenced by folk art appliqué patterns, it became so popular in France that decorative papers were specially printed for this purpose. Recently, decoupage has again become a favorite paper craft.

PHOTOMONTAGE (decoupage using photographs) is a more recent variation of collage. Cutting up and assembling photographs can be more than the mere assembly of images. By placing them in a certain way and on a particular surface, they may take on further and deeper meaning.

When you place paper over a raised surface and rub it with a crayon or chalk to make a drawing, it is called **FROTTAGE**. Similarly, passing paper through smoke can also have unusual effects—this technique is called **FUMAGE**.

French for "chewed paper," **PAPIER-MÂCHÉ** is the technique of molding scraps or flakes of paper mixed with glue into a three-dimensional shape. Papier-mâché is a simple technique that requires torn, mashed, or pulped paper and a dilute solution of water-based glue. The paper is dipped or soaked in the glue and applied piece by piece to an armature, or mold. The choice of paper and the thickness of the layers will determine the strength and finish of your piece. All kinds of projects are possible, from the simplest casting of a household plate to complex sculptural shapes. You can find your armature in nature or build a basic shape out of household materials such as wire, sticks, and cardboard.

At the beginning of each project in this kit, you'll find a list (entitled "You'll use") of materials, included here, that you will need to complete that project. Most of the papers included in this kit have preprinted templates on their back sides. The first time you make each project, you'll just need to match the paper color or pattern specified for that project (like this: ● ●) with the loose paper in the kit. Once you've used up the preprinted paper, you can use the templates at the back of this book (starting on page 69) to make more projects. Simply photocopy the templates onto the paper you'd like to use (enlarging as per the directions if necessary). And for three projects (the pinwheel, the box, and the garland), you'll find plastic templates in this kit that will allow you to skip the photocopying step altogether and trace the shapes directly onto your desired paper.

In addition to the materials included here (the assorted papers, the templates, the scoring/folding tool, and the dowels), you will need some simple tools to help you on your way. They may be things you already have at home, but they are also readily available in craft or art-supply stores. For each project, these items are listed under the heading "You'll also need":

- Scissors
- Craft utility (X-Acto™) knife
- Glue (traditional craft glue, like Elmer's™, is fine) or glue stick
- Pencil

- Ruler
- Sewing needle and thread
- Kite string
- Pushpins
- Ribbon

projects

wallet

Wallets are not only for our money and driver's license, but are also a classic way to store and carry special items, such as a photograph or an important message. Wallets traditionally fit in a bag or pocket but can also be large enough for a standard-sized document.

This project is a good introduction to the basic methods of paper craft. With a few folds and flaps, a sheet of paper becomes a wallet for your purse or coat pocket, or it can be folded to fit in your back pocket.

Feel free to be creative and give your wallet a personal touch by shaping the flap closure in your own way, or adding stickers or decorations to the outside. You can also turn your wallet into a present by slipping tickets or a gift certificate inside and closing it with a ribbon.

DIRECTIONS		
	1	Cut out panel A and score along the dotted lines. (fig. 1)
	2	Fold in the side flaps, then fold over the top flap and glue it to the side flaps. You have now created the basic wallet. (fig. 2)
	3	Next, cut out panel B and score along the dotted lines. (fig. 3)
	4	Fold in the three flaps. (fig. 4)
	5	Glue panel B to panel A, aligning their bottom edges as shown. (fig. 5)
	6	Your wallet now has two compartments, and can be closed using the top flap of panel A. (fig. 6)

You can also fold your wallet in the middle so it fits easily into your pocket.

FIGURE 1

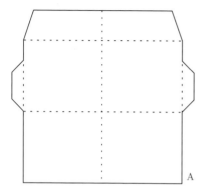

A

FIGURE 2

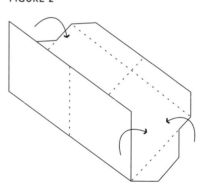

FIGURE 3

B

FIGURE 4

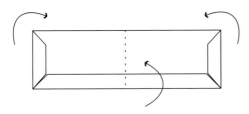

FIGURE 5

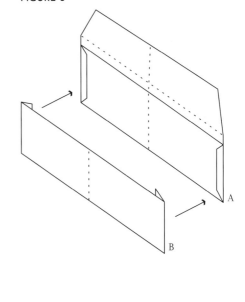

A

B

FIGURE 6

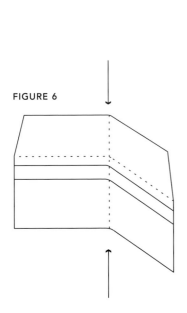

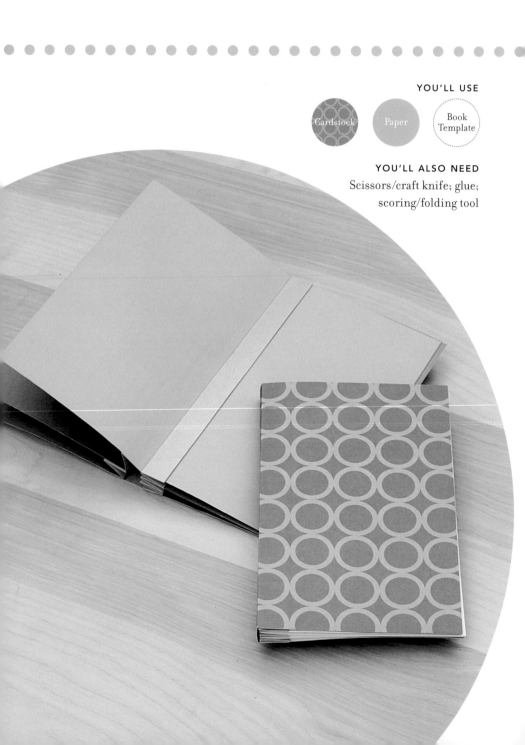

YOU'LL USE

Cardstock   Paper   Book Template

YOU'LL ALSO NEED
Scissors/craft knife; glue;
scoring/folding tool

book

For generations, books have been instrumental in accumulating and organizing similar thoughts and ideas into a single document. Binding sheets of written material together preserved ancient wisdom, information, and sacred texts. Different binding methods have been used in different parts of the world. For example, in ancient India and Southeast Asia, palm leaves were cut and tied together with string or leather strips and folded in an accordion-like, or "concertina," fashion. Words and pictures were scratched out on their pages with sharp pins and then rubbed with ink or concentrated dyes.

This project uses the concertina fold as the spine for you to construct your book. Once you have made your cover and spine, you will easily be able to add the pages.

Make a blank book to write in later, or decorate your pages in creative personalized ways using collage and other methods, and insert them into the spine once they are finished.

DIRECTIONS

1. Cut out cover panel A and score along the dotted lines. *(fig. 1)*

2. Fold the cover sheet, creating the spine for your book. *(fig. 2)*

3. Cut out spine sheet B and score along the dotted and dashed lines. *(fig. 3)*

4. Fold the sheet into a concertina, which will be inserted into the centerfold of the cover (fold in on the dotted lines and fold out on the dashed lines). *(fig. 4)*

5. Place glue along the outside flaps of the concertina. Making sure it is vertical to the cover, insert the concertina into the cover so the end flaps of the concertina line up with the spine. Glue it down. *(fig. 5)*

6   Close the book and press firmly along the outside flaps of the spine to affix it to the cover.

7   You now have the frame for your book. To make the pages, glue pieces of paper to each of the folds of the concertina. Cut pages to 4 3/4 x 8 inches to fit the cover exactly, or experiment with different sizes and shapes of paper for a more rustic look.

This simple book is a great beginning for lots of ideas. You can make a little album of photographs, drawings, or collage, or even make a story out of a sequence of pictures. If you like, you can add endpapers to the inside of the cover pages for more visual interest.

FIGURE 1

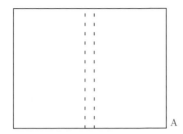

A

FIGURE 2

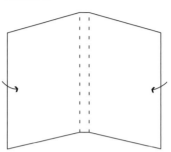

FIGURE 3

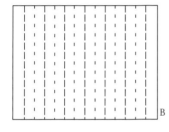

B

FIGURE 4

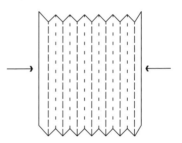

FIGURE 5

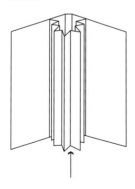

rosebud

● ●

Origami is at the heart of this project. The simple act of folding a flat piece of paper and turning it into a three-dimensional shape is the basis for an endless range of possibilities. The art of wrapping objects with paper, whether gifts or merely some groceries, is rooted in origami and has led to the creation of dazzling and complex sculptures made from folded paper. This expansion of origami's original function has brought wonder and delight through its decorative potential.

In this project you will begin with a square piece of paper and, as you fold and fold, watch as it takes on a new form, finally growing into a beautiful rosebud.

Your rosebud will be attractive just as an ornament, but insert a candle into the middle and you have a beautiful table decoration. Decorate a hat with it, attach it to a gift, or, using several buds, create a centerpiece for your next dinner party.

DIRECTIONS

1   Cut out your rosebud shape. Fold sharply along the indicated fold lines: Fold in on the dotted lines and fold out on the dashed lines, making a sharp crease along each fold line and the releasing it. *(fig. 1)*

2   After you've creased along all the lines, the paper should naturally fold into a circular shape. Continue following this shape, folding and pressing the paper tighter around the center. *(fig. 2)*

3   As the rosebud begins to appear, gently roll it into its final closed shape. *(fig. 3)*

4   Fold the four bottom corners or tabs to complete the flower and make its base. *(fig. 4)*

Your rosebud will look good in lots of colors; try black or metallics for a more sophisticated look! Try mixing several different colored buds together for a memorable decoration.

YOU'LL ALSO NEED
Scissors/craft knife;
scoring/folding tool

FIGURE 1

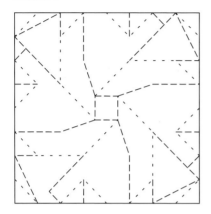

FIGURE 2

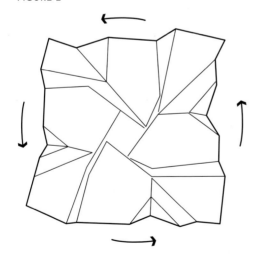

FIGURE 3

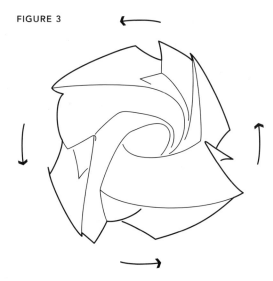

FIGURE 4

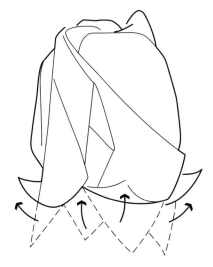

Note: Each piece of this paper will make 2 flowers, one large and one small.
Use all the papers to make enough flowers for your garland.

garland

Flowers are universal decorations, representing all kinds of sentiments. Strung together they become draping garlands or looping chains perfect to dress up or commemorate any occasion. For example, Hawaiians welcome and honor friends and guests by hanging garlands around their necks.

Paper flowers can appear very complex but often have a simple and beautiful symmetry to their design. In this project, by piecing together four shapes, twisting them in the right way, and gluing them together, you will make an 8-petal flower perfect for a garland. Once you get the hang of building these paper flowers, you will quickly be able to make a plethora of them and create wonderful garlands and flower chains of your own color scheme and design!

DIRECTIONS

1.   I. Cut out the petal shapes A and B and their two slits from the template provided.
II. Score and fold back segments A_1 and A_2 on either side of the slit in opposite directions. Repeat for petal B. *(fig. 1)*

2.   Glue segment A_1 and B_1 together, and segment A_2 and B_2 together. The shapes of the petals you glue together should match up, and the spherical shape of your flower should now be evident. *(fig. 2)*

3.   Cut out petal shapes C and D, and score and fold back the segments C_1 and C_2 on either side of the slot in opposite directions. Repeat for petal D. *(fig. 3)*

4.   Hold petals AB as shown *(fig. 4)* and slide petal C into place so the colors and/or patterns of each quadrant match up, and glue into place. Repeat for petal D. *(fig. 5)*

5.   Repeat steps 1 through 4 to make additional flowers. To make a garland you will need a needle and strong thread. Thread your needle, knot the end of the thread, and pierce it through the center of a flower. Pull the thread through to the knot, pierce your next flower in the same way and pull the thread through

again. When you have all your flowers on the thread, pull them close together and tie off the thread to create your garland.

Garlands can come in all lengths. You can make enough of these flowers to turn into a crown for a spring outfit, or add a few in with some standard paper streamers for a personal and unique party look. Mix lots of colors and try some different types of paper as you get more confident with garland-making.

FIGURE 1

FIGURE 2

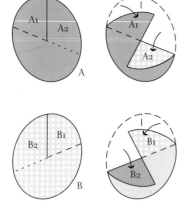

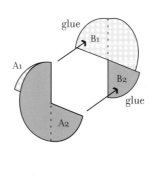

FIGURE 3

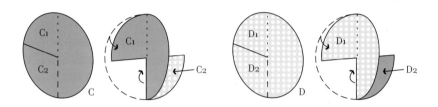

FIGURE 4

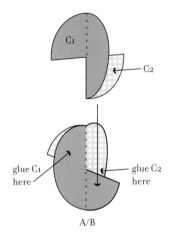

FIGURE 5

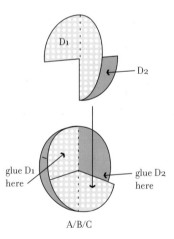

YOU'LL USE

YOU'LL ALSO NEED

Scissors/craft knife; glue; scoring/folding tool;
two dowels; needle with large eye; 10 yards kite string;
ribbons or streamers for decoration

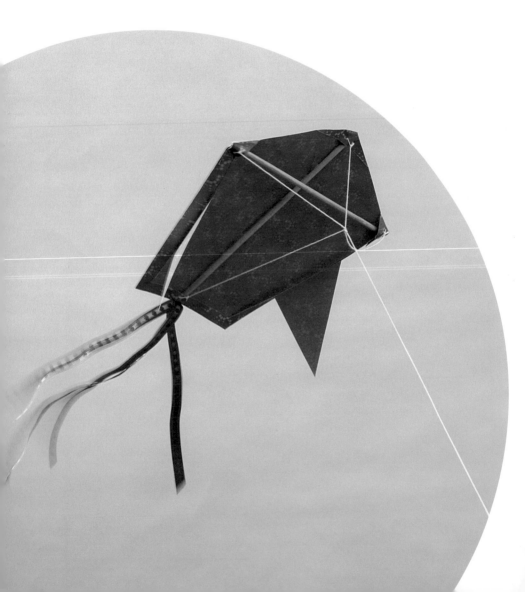

kite

Kites were created to simulate the magic of flight. In ancient Asia, kites were ubiquitous, and were even used in battle. The *Tako*, or Japanese fighting kite, could be so large that up to 40 men were needed to fly it! At royal spectacles kites would fill the sky, creating wonderful displays of color and movement.

The simple principle of dynamic airflow against a surface has been the inspiration of kite enthusiasts the world over for centuries. Many inventive designs were created based on interpretations of this principle, including box shapes, dragons, and multiple-winged kites. The simple kite you will build in this project, with paper stretched and supported on a light frame, is the basis of all these designs.

DIRECTIONS

1. Cut out your kite pattern, and score along the dashed and dotted lines. *(fig. 1)*

2. Fold in the two side flaps along the fold lines. *(fig. 2)*

3. I. Fold out the two wings along their fold lines.
   II. Fold in and glue down the bottom flap, leaving an unglued strip about ½-inch wide at the center for the vertical strut of your kite.
   III. Cut the vertical dowel to 8¾ inches using scissors or a craft knife. Place the dowel vertically in the center of the kite, and tuck one end into the bottom pocket created in step 3ii.
   IV. Now cut the horizontal dowel to 10¼ inches and place it on top of the vertical dowel at a 90-degree angle. Tuck each end of the horizontal dowel into the side flaps (formed in step 2) at the top left and right corners, just below the letters B and A. *(fig. 3)*

4. I. Fold down the top corner flaps (just above the letters B and A) and glue them to the side flaps. This will lock in the horizontal dowel.

II. Fold down the two flaps at the top of the kite, gluing one on top of the other. This will lock in the vertical dowel. *(fig. 4)*

5 I. Using your needle, pierce the kite in eight places on the back flaps: above and below the dowel on corner A, above and below the dowel on corner B, to the left and right of the dowel at point C, and to the left and right of the dowel at point D. These are the holes through which you'll thread your kite string connectors.

II. Cut two lengths of kite string, each 15 inches long. Thread your needle with one length, and loop it down through one of the holes on corner A, under the dowel, and up through the other hole on corner A. Tie off the string into a knot *(fig. 5)*. Repeat with the holes on corner B. When you finish, pull up the excess string; it should measure about three inches up from the kite. Repeat the process for points C and D.

III. Now tie one end of your kite string at the meeting point between the two strings. *(fig. 6)*

Once you have completed the kite construction and your string is attached, you will need to add a tail to stabilize and decorate your kite. For this you can add 4 to 6 paper streamers or ribbons to the base corner of your kite. See if you have some leftover paper streamers or gift ribbons. If not, you can cut perfect streamers from a roll of crepe paper. Your tails should be around two feet long. If you choose to make them longer, they may affect the flight of your kite. If this happens, gradually trim the tails until they provide the proper degree of stabilization.

Once your kite is made, put it to the test! Ask a friend to hold your kite up high in the breeze, letting the wind fill its belly. Hold the string taut and start to run as your friend throws it aloft. It may take a few attempts to catch the wind, but once it stays up, slowly let out the string, continuing to keep it taut as your kite rises into the sky. Happy flying!

FIGURE 1

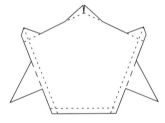

FIGURE 2

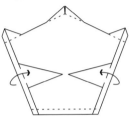

FIGURE 3

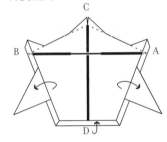

FIGURE 4

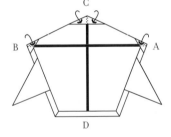

FIGURE 5

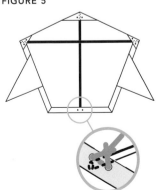

FIGURE 6

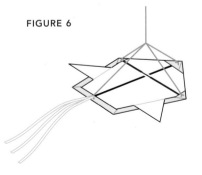

pop-up display card & envelope

Traditionally, greeting cards come folded with a picture or message on the outside. The fold creates a hinge, which is also the basis for most pop-up designs. As a pop-up card opens, folded paper emerges from the inside and transforms into a three-dimensional shape.

Pop-up design has evolved into a wide-range of methods and complexities over its 400-year history, but this pop-up project keeps things simple. The basic pop-up mechanism of this project opens out and turns into a display or easel for a photograph or picture framed by a window. An envelope, which has a unique four-fold closure, is included as part of this project to complement your card.

You can write a message on the inside or outside of the card, and can decorate all sides of the card to deliver your message in a creative and beautiful way.

CARD

DIRECTIONS

1   Cut out Panel A for the back part of your pop-up display card. *(fig. 1)*

2   Score along the dotted line and fold. *(fig. 2)*

3   Cut out Panel B for the front of your pop-up display card, including the oval window and two slots. *(fig. 3)*

4   Score along the dotted and dashed lines and fold out along the centerline. Fold in the two end flaps. *(fig. 4)*

5   Write a message and decorate the front panel of your display card however you wish. Match the end flaps of the front panel to the outside edges of the back panel, and glue the two panels together along these flaps. *(fig. 5)*

Cardstock   Cardstock   Vellum   Card Template   Envelope Template

6 Now slide your photograph into the slots in the front panel and your pop-up display card is ready to go! *(fig. 6)*

In order to put your card and photograph in the envelope, remove the photograph from the card, fold the card inward, and place the card and photo separately in the envelope.

FIGURE 1

FIGURE 2

FIGURE 3

FIGURE 4

FIGURE 5

FIGURE 6

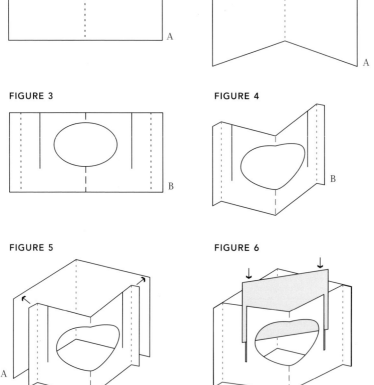

ENVELOPE

DIRECTIONS

1   Cut out your envelope and score along the dotted lines. *(fig. 1)*

2   Fold the petal flaps over in a clockwise order. *(figs. 2 & 3)*

3   As you fold the fourth and final flap, lift the first flap so that it overlaps the fourth flap. This will close the envelope. *(fig. 4)*

Family snapshots, an image of a sweetheart, or even some nostalgic pictures— you can put whatever you want in this card. Pick your photograph or image to display and then decorate the card to dramatize the effect. You can draw with colored crayons or markers, use decorative stickers, or even collage for a personal feel.

FIGURE 1

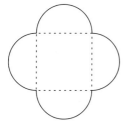

FIGURE 2

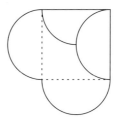

FIGURE 3

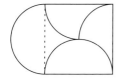

FIGURE 4

YOU'LL USE

Box Template

Cardstock

YOU'LL ALSO NEED

Scissors/craft knife;
scoring/folding tool

box

Hardly a day goes by that we don't find ourselves using one type of box or another. We find much of our everyday things stored in some kind of box, from our breakfast cereal to the personal files we store at the back of the garage. Boxes are usually rectangular for easy construction and to most efficiently house their contents, but they also come in other shapes that in some way reflect the form of the object inside. The box you make with this project could be used for a small gift, keepsake, or jewelry.

Once you've mastered the assembly of this fundamental box design, try using this pattern with different types of paper. Also, if you paint or decorate the four flaps of the template in different patterns, they will come together in an interesting way when you fold up and close the box.

DIRECTIONS	1	Cut out your box shape and score along the fold lines. *(fig. 1)*
	2	Fold over and interlock flaps A and B. *(fig. 2)*
	3	Fold over the last two flaps and interlock them to complete your box. *(fig. 3)*

How about a box set? Photocopy the template three times, magnifying the size 20 percent each time. When you have made these different sized boxes, they will fit inside each other.

FIGURE 1

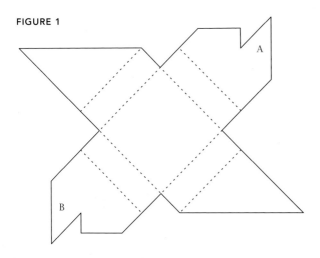

FIGURE 2

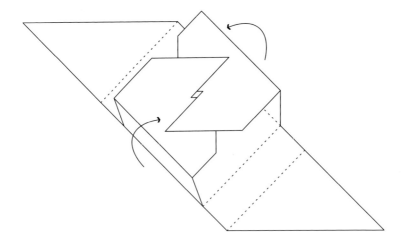

FIGURE 3

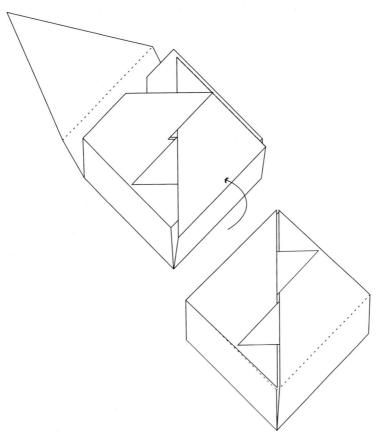

YOU'LL USE

Lantern
Template

Vellum

YOU'LL ALSO NEED

Scissors/craft knife; scoring/folding tool; three dowels

lantern

· ·

When light shines through paper, there is a beautiful and mysterious effect created that brings a warm and welcome feeling. By placing paper around a light source to create a lantern, it gives an even glow. For this reason, paper is often used in lanterns, particularly in Asia. The famous sculptor Isamu Noguchi created many beautifully shaped lamps, based on this effect, after noticing the lanterns of fishermen in Japan. These lamps, made of paper glued onto cane rings for strength, emitted a beautiful light when in use, but then could be compressed flat for storage.

The lantern you will build in this project has three sticks, or dowels, that hold it together, allow it to stand upright, and, like the lanterns of Noguchi's Japanese fishermen, enable it to be folded and stored flat.

In addition, the cutout holes in the panels of the lantern add a decorative effect, which may suggest other creative possibilities to you. Try cutting out different shapes and designs from some translucent paper, like tissue or vellum, or layering and folding these papers in different ways and then holding them up to a light or to a window.

DIRECTIONS

1   Cut out the lantern shade and the six squares of the lantern. Also, cut along the slit lines in each panel to make the opening for the dowels. *(fig. 1)*

2   Score lightly along the dotted lines and fold the lantern into a triangle, overlapping the end flaps, keeping flap D on top of flap A. *(fig. 2)*

3   Line up the slits of flaps A and D. Feed the first dowel through the top slits (going through both flaps) and slide it down through the middle and bottom slits (going through both flaps). *(fig. 3)*

4   Slide the other two dowels through the slits on flaps B and C. *(fig. 4)*

You now have your lantern shade which stands on its three dowel legs. The lantern can now be placed over and around a candle or another light source. You can raise or lower the paper shade on these legs to suit the height of your candle or to create an effect you like. To store your lantern, simply remove the dowels and fold up your lantern shade.

The effect of light through paper is always fascinating, whether it's the type of paper you use or the shapes you cut out of it. You can vary the paper and cutout holes in this project and make a whole collection of holiday decorations or gifts.

⚠ Caution: Never leave a burning candle unattended. Take care to ensure that any candle you use is a safe distance away from the paper of the lantern so as not to set it on fire.

FIGURE 1

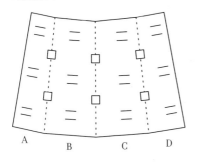

A   B   C   D

FIGURE 2

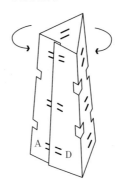

FIGURE 3

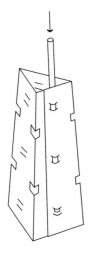

FIGURE 4

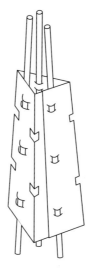

pinwheel

The pinwheel is a favorite toy that can be found in festivals around the world. As old as kites, these little wind machines are handheld models of windmills and their propellers. Children love to play with these clever devices, watching the magic as wind turns this simple shape into a whirring delight.

The pinwheel lends itself to all kinds of decoration, from painting and coloring to streamers and whistles. With creative planning, your designs may be enhanced by movement. For example, if you paint the tips of your pinwheel with the same color, the colored tips will form the illusion of a circle when the wheel is in motion. Painting another solid color in a circle at the center of the pinwheel will add even more to this mesmerizing effect.

DIRECTIONS

1. Cut out the pinwheel shape. *(fig. 1)*
2. Fold over the first sail, aligning the tip of the sail onto the mark at the center of the pinwheel. Affix the sail together at these marks with a spot of glue, and wait for the glue to dry. *(fig. 2)*
3. Continue folding and fixing the other three sails in a clockwise direction, gluing each sail at the center after the previous spot of glue is dry. *(fig. 3)*
4. You are now ready to attach your pinwheel to its mast. Piercing the front of the pinwheel at the center with a pushpin, pin the wheel to the dowel. Be sure to leave enough space between the head of the pushpin and the dowel for the wheel to turn freely.

Hold your pinwheel up into a breeze; slowly turn the wheel until it catches the wind and begins to spin on its own and *voilà*! Instant pinwheel-fun! If you use a longer pin, like a carpenter's nail or dress pin, you can have two wheels on one stick.

Paper Pinwheel Template

FIGURE 1

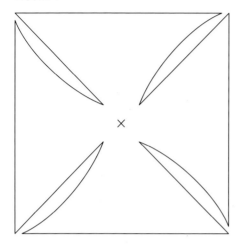

FIGURE 2

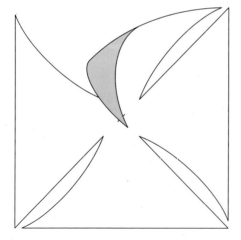

FIGURE 3

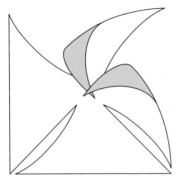

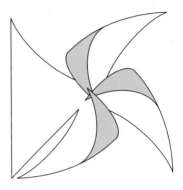

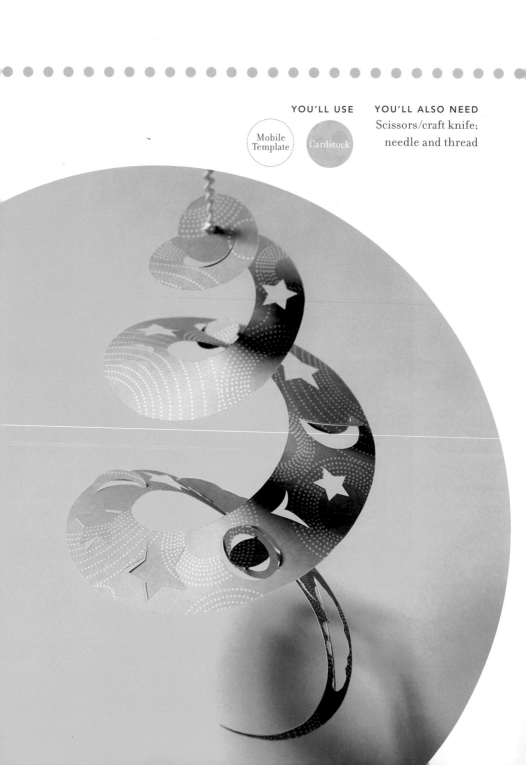

mobile

For those familiar with this modern art form, the word *mobile* probably conjures up pictures of the graceful moving sculptures of Alexander Calder. These kinetic constructions of the modern art world seemed unique to their time. However, hanging decorations that turn in the air are rooted in the folk-craft traditions of many cultures. These traditional toys often would be a simple wheel on which various objects could hang. Little toy figures, animals, or other shapes created a design, told a story, or recounted a mythical legend. These characters, turning in a circle, may have been the origin of moving optical machines and possibly even movies!

You will notice the spiral design used in this project is a shape that is both two- and three-dimensional. When you cut out the mobile and hang it, the spiral reveals its form, looking like it is both coiling and uncoiling as it turns.

In this project, you can enhance the decoration of your mobile by coloring the various stars and planets in the template before you begin to cut out the design.

DIRECTIONS

1 Cut out the spiral mobile shape. *(fig. 1)*

2 Carefully cut out the clouds, stars, and planets, leaving the tabs that connect them to the mobile. It is best to use a craft knife to cut out shapes this small.

3 Press out and gently rotate these cut out shapes so they are at 90-degree angles to the mobile. *(fig. 2)*

4 Holding the mobile at its center, let it drop to reveal its spiral shape. *(fig. 3)*

You can now hang the mobile from the ceiling by a lightweight string *(fig. 3)* or suspend it from a dowel. Your mobile is a delightful toy to hang near a child's bed or over a baby's crib, bringing a restful, relaxed feeling to the room.

FIGURE 1

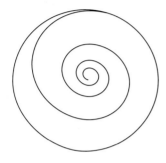

FIGURE 2

FIGURE 3

resources

Books

These are just a few of the many excellent books that inform and inspire the world of paper craft. Your local library or bookstore may have some of these titles, while good-quality used or new copies are available from online bookstores.

Baskett, Mickey. *Creative Paper Folding*. New York: Sterling Publishing Co., Inc., 2002.

Christensen, Mimi. *The New Paper Style*. New York: Sterling/Chapelle, 2002.

Couzins-Scott, Elizabeth, M. Elliot, M. Maguire, and S. Walton. *Papercraft Workshop: Over 100 Inspirational Papercrafting Projects*. London: Southwater Publishing, 2004.

Genovese, Sandi. *Creative Greeting Cards*. New York: Sterling Publishing Co., Inc., 2001.

LaPlantz, Shereen. *Cover to Cover: Creative Techniques for Making Beautiful Books, Journals & Albums*. New York: Lark Books, 1998.

Maurer-Mathison, Diane, and J. Philippoff. *Paper Art: The Complete Guide to Paper Craft Techniques*. New York: Watson-Guptill Publications, 1997.

Souter, Gillian. *Paper Crafts: 50 Extraordinary Gifts and Projects Step by Step*. New York: Random House Value Publishing, 1995.

Welch, Nancy. *Creative Paper Art: Techniques for Transforming the Surface*. New York: Sterling Publishing Company, Inc., 2000.

Magazines

Magazines come and go, but here are some helpful and informative magazines that are in print at the time of this writing.

Paper Crafts
Paper Works
Card Making & Papercraft
Papercraft Inspirations
Crafts-Beautiful

Online References

The Internet is an amazing source of reference for almost all subjects. Paper and its craft often come as part of general craft sources, but with some creative searching there is much to find. You can sometimes even find free downloads of templates and other craft tools.

www.cardmakingandpapercraft.com/downloads.asp
www.papercraftz.com
www.allcrafts.net
www.yasutomo.com

Online Suppliers and Mail Order

You can find all your materials and often much more on the Internet. Most Web sites have comprehensive catalogs to help you choose. However, when shopping on the Internet you won't be able to touch the papers, so their quality and feel, which is so important in paper craft, won't be apparent before you buy. Here are some sites that you may find useful as you explore your craft.

www.samflax.com
www.artstore.com
www.handmade-paper.us
www.dickblick.com
www.michaels.com
www.craft-search.com
www.paperzone.com

www.indiamart.com
www.papermojo.com
www.nepalesepaper.com

Paper and Craft Stores

Most arts and crafts stores are local businesses, so look in your local yellow pages or directory to find one near you. It is good to touch and feel paper when making your purchasing decisions, so buying your supplies directly from a store has its advantages over mail order.

Here are some well-known stores carrying paper and craft supplies that have branches state- or nationwide.

Flax (www.flaxart.com)
Utrecht (www.utrecht.com)
The Art Store (www.artstore.com)
Amsterdam Art (www.amsterdamart.com)
Papyrus (www.papyrus.com)

Additional References

Barrett, Timothy. *Japanese Papermaking: Traditions, Tools, and Techniques*. New York: Weatherhill, 1992.

Cohn, Angelo. *Wonderful World of Paper*. London and New York: Abelard-Schuman, Ltd., 1967.

Dawson, Sophie. *The Art and Craft of Papermaking: Step by Step Instructions for Creating Distinctive Handmade Paper*. New York: Lark Books, 1997.

Jackson, Paul. *Encyclopedia of Origami and Papercraft Techniques*. Philadelphia: Running Press, 1991.

____. *The Pop-Up Book: Step-By-Step Instructions for Creating over 100 Original Paper Projects*. New York: Henry Holt & Co., 1994.

Japan Craft Forum. *Japanese Crafts: A Complete Guide to Today's Traditional Handmade Objects*. Tokyo: Kodansha International, 2001.

Limousin, Odile. *The Story of Paper: What is Paper Made Of?* New York: Young Discovery Library, 1988.

Newman, Thelma, J. Newman, and L.S. Newman. *Paper As Art and Craft: The Complete Book of History and Processes of the Paper Arts*. New York: Crown Publishers, 1973.

Saint-Gilles, Amaury. *Mingei: Japan's Enduring Folk Arts*. Rutland, VT: Tuttle Publishing, 1989.

Shannon, Faith. *The Art and Craft of Paper*. San Francisco: Chronicle Books, 1994.

Weaver, Alexander. *Paper, Wasps & Packages: The Romantic Story of Paper and Its Influence on the Course of History*. Chicago: Container Corporation of America, 1937.

Ziegler, Kathleen and N. Greco. *Paper Sculpture: A Step-By-Step Guide*. Rockport, MA: Rockport Publishers, Inc., 1996.

www.emile.co.jp/awagami
www.kansai.gr.jp
www.artonpaper.com
www.encyclopedia.com

templates

wallet

Please enlarge this template to 200% on a photocopier.

A

B

book, cover

Please enlarge this template to 200% on a photocopier.

A

book, spine

Please enlarge this template to 200% on a photocopier.

B

rosebud

Please enlarge this template to 200% on a photocopier.

garland

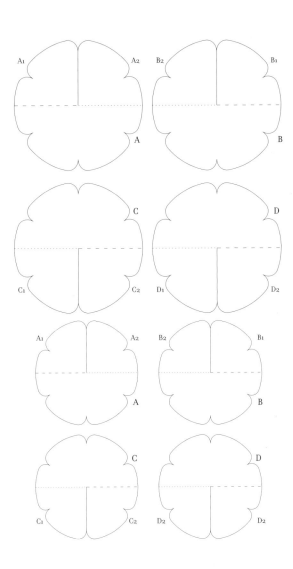

kite

Please enlarge this template to 250% on a photocopier.

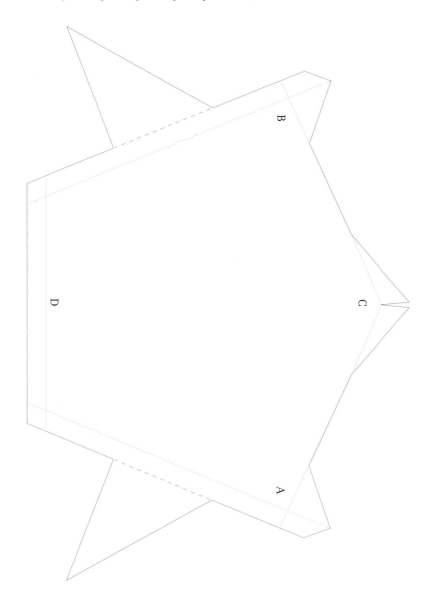

pop-up display card

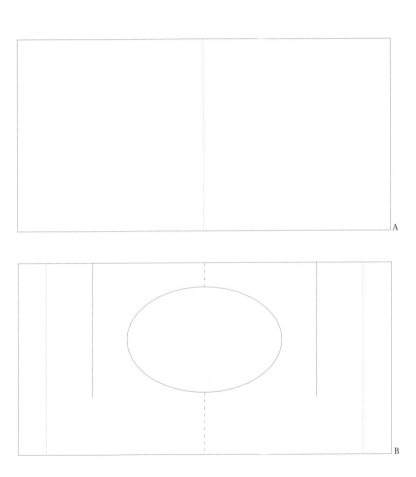

envelope

Please enlarge this template to 250% on a photocopier.

box

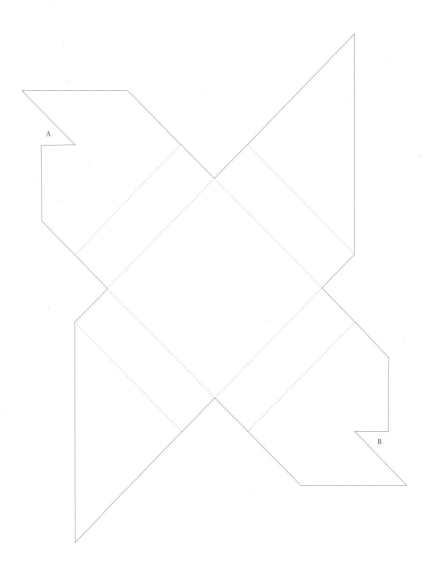

lantern

Please enlarge this template to 200% on a photocopier.

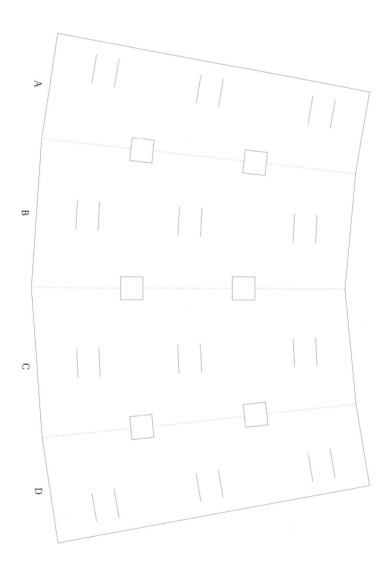

pinwheel

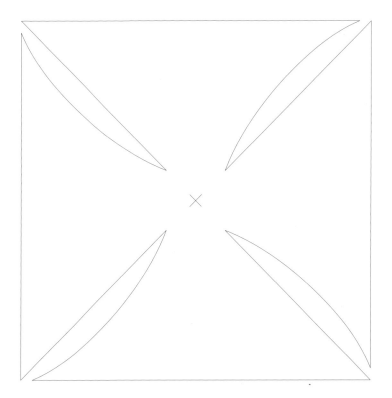

mobile

Please enlarge this template to 200% on a photocopier.

This template leaves out the moon, star, and cloud shapes of the original project (see page 60). This way, you can make very basic mobiles, or use the stencil included with this kit to add cutouts to your mobile. If you add cutout shapes, remember to leave small tabs to connect the shapes to your mobile for the 3-D effect.

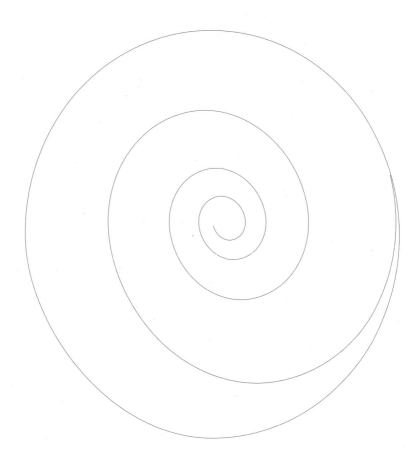